The Short Cheap Tax Book for Students

50 Plus Things to Get Young People's Tax and Financial Life Started Off Right

Kirk Taylor

Copyright 2019 Kirk Taylor

To the extent that this book uses specific numbers, they are for the 2019 tax year. I will update each year, but the book is designed such that you don't need to get a new copy every year (but it's cheap, so do it anyway, that way I know you love me!)

This is the fifth book in The Short Cheap Tax Book series. These books are meant to expound upon the information on my blog: supertaxgenius.blogspot.com (Link #1) and from my other books in a targeted, specific and snarky way. My blog is meant for generic, public consumption at no charge. This book you pay for, so you get my very unvarnished, very uncensored opinions.

For those of you listening to the audiobook, there is a pdf file you can download that has the website links referenced here in a way that you can click on them and go directly to the source. They will be numbered to correspond to the links in the text.

The impetus for this book is that, after 25 years in the Navy, 20 years doing taxes, and a couple of years as a financial advisor, I went to college for the first time. Now in the past, I had taken a lot of courses, classes and tests, both in and out of the Navy, and I have done a ton of teaching and curriculum development, but I had never sat in a formal college classroom. To say it was eye opening for a 50-year-old, grizzled military vet would be an understatement. This book takes the lessons I learned as a Navy Nuclear Submarine Master Chief, Tax Expert, Old Experienced Dude and Novice College Student and distills them down to some practical, useful and easy to understand advice about life, college, finances and taxes.

The primary audience for this book is young men and women just getting started in life. I want it to help them to avoid some of the mistakes too many people make, and also get them started on smart life decisions that are best made while young. High School students, college students, trade school students, apprentices, young workers and also parents can all benefit from the chapters in this book.

A few of the chapters are similar to (or copied from) the Short Cheap Tax Book for Everyone, since learning these lessons while young is vitally important.

This book is way more than taxes – but I'm not an expert on the other areas, just experienced – it's an opinion book, not a reference book. You may not agree with me on everything I say, and some of it might be wrong – but give it a good read with an open mind and you will find things that help you.

If you find this book useful, you should consider at least two of my other books: The Short Cheap Tax Book for Everyone (Link #2) and Everyday Taxes (Link #3). Make sure to get the latest year of Everyday Taxes. The first has almost universally applicable great advice, and the second has dozens of chapters ordered around life events. The first is cheap, the second quite a bit more expensive because it has detailed information and takes months to write – so you're paying for the damage to my two typing fingers. That's right, everything in the books and on the blogs is written by a hunt and pecker.

DISCLAIMER:

Because lawyers suck and people are greedy, it is important to point out that this book represents MY opinions and interpretations, and are not necessarily those of the IRS or my employer. These chapters are short and sweet, so they don't cover all details and may not be accurate for your situation. Do your own research to be certain. Talk to a competent professional. Do not rely solely on this book. Also, client confidentiality is important, so the spirit of client stories is true, but the details are significantly altered. Also, to be clear, I am neither a currently licensed financial advisor, nor a mental health counselor of any kind.

Now Is a Good Time to Learn How Taxes Work

Everybody thinks they understand taxes, but very few people do. You don't have to become an expert, but you should understand the difference between a credit and a deduction (deductions reduce taxable income while credits reduce taxes – credits are better). You should understand that what is taken out of your paycheck is literally a GUESS as to how much taxes you owe (and you file a tax RETURN to get a REFUND of excess taxes paid or to determine how much you still OWE). You should realize that going up a tax bracket is a GOOD thing (you make more money, but the higher tax rate is only applied to your income above the new bracket).

There is a lot of other stuff that you should get familiar with, including how your paycheck works with regard to taxes, the fact that FICA taxes aren't part of your tax return (they are gone until you collect Social Security or go on Medicare), and that the Internal Revenue Service isn't as evil and powerful as they are made out to be (though you still don't want to piss them off).

Take some time to begin to understand how all this works, and you will be better for it as your life goes on.

The next chapter is a good place to start on this.

Download a Copy of the Federal and State Instruction Books

They're free. Put them on the back of the toilet and read them while you poop.

This is a great way to get familiar with what things you pay taxes on and what you can deduct. Walking through the instructions while looking at the forms gives you an idea how your taxes should be prepared, how the numbers on your W-2 translate into a tax amount, and give you an idea what your software should be spitting out.

You would be amazed at what you find there that might apply to you that your software forgets to mention. Remember, easy isn't accurate, and software tries hard to be easy. You might even find some deductions your tax guy missed! If you do, your tax guy should give you your money back and do the amendment for free - I would.

Have the books handy if you use software to file your taxes (or download a fresh copy if you're a germaphobe). These books also make quite powerful sleep aids - and they are definitely NOT habit forming.

Always Print a Copy of Your Tax Returns

What a stupid chapter! I mean, seriously, isn't this obvious?

Based on how often I'm asked to get someone a copy of their tax return in the middle of summer, no it is not. Print a copy, put it with all the supporting documents, and throw it in a safe place. I like one of those small, top opening file boxes. I keep stuffing the returns in until the new one doesn't fit, then I shred the oldest one. You should have 4 years at a minimum, but I probably have 7 to 10 years in there.

While you're at it, if you can get an electronic copy, save that on your computer, and your backup hard drive, and maybe even a floppy disk (ask your Dad if you don't know what that is). When you move, these files go with YOU, not in the moving van.

Let me add that, a little time spent anywhere that people ask tax questions (God help me, Reddit is a cesspool of tax ignorance), will enlighten you that needing information from a prior year tax return is the absolute most common tax topic. You can't even e-file your current tax return without knowing your prior year Adjusted Gross Income (AGI). Most people don't know this because their software remembers it for them and/or a professional doesn't need it. Need to file FASFA, or buy a house – you're gonna need that tax return. And that letter from the IRS…good luck if you can't find the tax return.

Update Your Address with the IRS and Your State

I know these first few chapters are going to make it seem like this book is filled with a bunch of really obvious stuff, BUT, these chapters are based on REAL LIFE. At least 25% of all the tax problems I'm asked to help with wouldn't have happened, or would be a lot easier to handle if these first few pieces of advice were followed. So…Update your address with the IRS…

EVERY TIME YOU MOVE!

Believe it or not, the IRS doesn't automatically know that you've moved, and the U.S. Postal Service is not competent enough to trust that a Change of Address form will work. The IRS sends letters to the address on your tax return if you haven't changed it using the IRS website. If the letter suggests a change to your tax return, the clock starts ticking on disputing it as soon as they send it. Updating the IRS when you move will save you a TON of heartache. This happens way too often, and is way too easy to prevent.

Here's an IRS site with more information:
https://www.irs.gov/taxtopics/tc157.html (Link #4)

You're on your own for the state, but their Revenue Department website should make it easy.

This year I had three clients who were getting ID theft PINs from the IRS and didn't update their address. There is almost no way to fix this and avoid having to paper file.

If you are going to college, joining the military or moving around a lot, you might want to use your parent's address until you are settled.

Don't Fear the IRS

If you're not cheating, you have very little to worry about beyond money and hassle. Professionals like to scare you with the IRS, and, if you're cheating, you should be scared. I prefer to scare people with the prospect of not getting all they deserve.

Let's put it this way: Say you've got a nice desk to donate to charity. You check some stores and eBay, and the values are between $500 and $1000 dollars. Assuming the $1000 isn't a huge outlier, that is 5 sites between $500 and $550 and one at $1000, take the $1000. It's reasonable, defensible, and not frivolous. If you're in the 22% tax bracket, that's $110 on your tax return, plus some from the State! Now let's say the mean old IRS does its worst, and face to face audits you. The auditor looks at your documents and tells you the desk's only worth $500. You argue a bit, but he insists, and you have to pay back the $110, plus a bit of interest. No handcuffs, no jail-time, no yelling or beatings. You shake hands, sign some paperwork and write a check. Now let's pretend we're in Vegas. You find a table that gives you $110, and then spins a wheel, and if you lose you have to give them the $110 back, plus $15, except you only lose 1 out of 100 times! Who wouldn't make that bet? That's the same thing we're talking about with the desk.

JUST DON'T CHEAT!

Don't Lie to the IRS

Don't ignore them either.

Exaggerate, stretch, manipulate, but don't lie. Two things the IRS hates more than anything, being lied to and being ignored. They're like your Mom. I encourage taking the most aggressive tax position you can that's not a lie or frivolous.

Do be aware that if you get aggressive, you need to be prepared to lose in a fight with the IRS. Know how much money you're risking by being aggressive, and be prepared to pay some or all of it back at a later date. Odds are you'll get to keep the money, but it's good to be prepared.

Not lying is a good habit to get into generally. Some times it seems like lying is easier, but keeping your lies straight is harder than just telling the truth.

Man, I'm starting to sound like a sanctimonious gasbag!

Don't Do Things Just for The Tax Benefit

There are very few things that will improve your taxes without costing you in other areas of your life. You only get a portion of any deduction off your taxes, so often times not paying something is better than getting the deduction.

People who tell you not to pay off your home mortgage because it's your best tax deduction are just stupid. You pay $10,000 in interest to get $2200 back on your taxes (22% tax bracket). BRILLIANT! You're out $7800. Of course, the tax benefit combined with other realities (like you don't have $200,000 to pay the mortgage off or you have better things to do with the money) can make this a smart idea, but don't just do it for the taxes.

As a point of fact, most things that are good for your taxes, you actually do for better, non-tax reasons:

Health Savings Account? For your health.
401k or IRA? For your future.
Kids? Seriously, if you're having kids for the tax benefits, you are doing it wrong. VERY WRONG.

Later, I will cover some cool things to do to save on taxes that don't hurt in real life, and cover some that hurt a little, but then I'll tell you how to make the decision the best way possible.

That's why you bought the book, right?

Don't Believe What You Hear About Taxes

Unless you hear about it from a competent professional that you trust, it's very likely to be crap information. Everybody thinks they know everything about everything, but most people are just repeating crap they heard that's wrong, or misinterpreting things they heard that were right.

Government websites are usually reliable.
Big financial publications (Kiplinger's for example) are pretty good.
Newspapers and broadcast news are terrible.
Blogs (other than mine), Facebook posts, friends, neighbors...all useless.

Competent tax professionals are the only people you should trust for sure.

You can't even trust IRS employees. Believe it or not, if you get an answer from the IRS over the phone, and it's wrong, it's still on you. You need it in writing for them to back themselves up, and that costs money.

I wrote myself a note to list the stupidest things about taxes I've heard, but there's just no room, and no way to pick a winner.

The Income Tax is Not Illegal

I'm not kidding.

All those people screaming about not filing taxes and getting away with it are full of dookie (though they may get away with it for a while because the IRS sucks at enforcement).

There are tons of examples of BS arguments: the 16th amendment was never properly ratified, taxes are voluntary, zero returns, wages aren't income...all CRAP.

The IRS will not only dismiss your attempt to argue this muck, but can actually fine you MORE (a lot more – up to $25,000) just for trying. They can also fine your tax guy or lawyer for arguing these things.

These situations have been thoroughly litigated, many all the way to the Supreme Court. The income tax is SETTLED LAW. Don't fall for these things.

The 7th Circuit Court of Appeals put it best: "Like moths to a flame, some people find themselves irresistibly drawn to the tax protester movement's illusory claim that there is no legal requirement to pay federal income tax. And, like moths, these people sometimes get burned." United States v. Sloan (7th Circuit 1991).

The IRS Didn't Call You

Unless you are currently involved in communications with the IRS that were initiated by you in person or by the IRS via a letter, that person calling claiming to be the "IRS" is full of you know what.

The IRS does NOT initiate communications via phone calls. Scammers trying to steal your money or identity do.

I have already had TONS of people (including me) receive these kinds of calls. If you want a little more reassurance, try googling the number the call came from (if the number is hidden it's DEFINETELY a scam). Chances are the google results will be full of people asking about the number, and MANY people identifying it as a scam. If you want more reassurance, call the IRS (though this is pretty much a waste of time during peak filing periods.)

These guys are professionals, and they can often sound very convincing, and will even threaten to arrest you. Swear at them and hang up.

Lately they have gotten more sophisticated and are even sending relatively real-looking letters. Always assume someone calling and asking for money or personal information is a scam – tax based or not. Independently look the agency's contact information up online and call direct.

If they ask you to pay with gift cards…it's a scam. Seriously, how do people think the IRS wants iTunes gift cards?

Pay Attention to Your Withholding

You should check every pay stub, every time, and make sure your withholding is consistent.

The amount coming out of your paycheck for taxes should stay the same if your pay stays the same, go up if your pay goes up, and go down if your pay goes down (obvious, I know). If you want to be extra careful, you can track your year to date withholding numbers and make sure it lines up with the prior year.

Payroll people sometimes make mistakes, so you need to keep an eye on this, and find out why if things change drastically. Don't just assume that everything is fine. Tax time is a bad time to find out something was wrong.

A couple years ago, I discovered halfway through tax season that my employer wasn't withholding ANY state taxes. I had to have them withhold ONE THOUSAND DOLLARS every two weeks for the rest of the season to make up the difference.

Don't Go Exempt!

Seriously!

This is one of the worst things you can do. Some workplaces that pay bonuses have people who go exempt on tax withholding just before bonus time, so they get the full amount of the bonus.

THIS IS LUNACY!

These people will try to convince you of how smart they are, and try to convince you to do it as well. DON'T! Tax time gets ugly when you do this, especially for the people who forget to change it back after they get the bonus. There is much wailing and gnashing of teeth at my tax desk when this happens - and I have NO sympathy.

The reason they withhold so much out of bonuses is that they skew the calculation of what your annual income will be, and can cause your regular wages to be seriously under withheld. You NEED the bonus withholding to keep you safe. If they over withhold you will get the extra money back when you file taxes.

Tax Software Sucks

Why does tax software suck? Simple: it has to be both user friendly, easy to use, and accurate. If it's not user friendly and easy to use, no one is going to pay for it. Hell, that's why it's so popular! It is simply not possible to cover all the complexities of tax law and still be easy to use. So, they make it easy to use: "How much did you pay for uniforms?" Sure, there's an info button you can click that will go into all the nitty gritty of this question, but if you read them every time they come up, it's not simple and easy anymore. "How many miles did you drive for business last year?" Again, many pop-ups will be available to help you navigate the dizzying rules that are involved in this simple question, but you're not likely to read them, and, if you do, they're only going to make you more confused. Don't even get me started on depreciation, business use of home, or investing income!

And that's just the Federal return!

Many states have nearly incomprehensible tax laws, and dozens of deductions and credits that you pretty much need to know exist in order to take advantage of them. Most software just drags things from the Federal to the State, with barely a peep about what deductions you might miss. I cannot even begin to describe the messes I've seen from tax software. Recently, a client with one W-2, no wife, no kids, no house, and an amazingly simple Federal 1040EZ missed out on over $10,000 in state tax money over the previous dozen years because either the software didn't ask, or he neglected to answer enough questions to establish that his military income was exempt from California taxes. Most of that money is gone forever.

Tax preparation software SUCKS! You will have a better chance at an accurate return using pen and paper with the Federal and State instructions than you will using software!

Who Gets to Claim You on Their Taxes?

Now we are getting to the specifics of being a student. For most students, the answer is your parent, though it can get more complicated as you get older. Putting it simply, if you live at home (or come home after the semester), don't make a lot of money and don't have a ton of student loans, your parents should be claiming you. Even if you do a lot of travel or spend a summer at school, they should usually still claim you.

If you permanently move out of your parent's home, starting before the middle of the year, they can generally no longer claim you. If YOU provide more than half of your own support, including tuition, you should be claiming yourself. Student loans you have to repay (as well as money you make and spend on yourself) count as support paid by you, but the fair rental value of your parent's home, utilities they pay, tuition they pay and all the food, clothes and other stuff they pay on your behalf count as paid by them. When you turn 24, your parent's have to pay more than half (before you just couldn't be paying more than half yourself). It's a very complicated situation, but also usually pretty obvious.

If it's not obvious, you and your parents should coordinate filing your taxes such that everyone knows what's being done. This should usually involve a professional, just to make sure.

In the IRS' eyes, there is only one correct answer to this, and it is usually a matter of math. They won't generally get fussy if it's close and there is no dispute between you and your parents.

If there are other relatives involved instead of parents, it USUALLY works out the same, but they should check with a pro. If there are non-relatives instead of parents, definitely get a pro involved.

There is No "Table"

So, you can't be paid "Under" it.

As a general rule, every dollar you make, especially if it is for providing goods or services is taxable. Just because you get paid in cash and there is no paperwork doesn't change this.

I'm not your ethics counselor, so I can't make you do something you don't want to, but I can tell you that the law is very clear on this, and if you decide not to declare income, the penalties can be very harsh.

I have seen, many times, where someone thinks they are being paid "under the table" when in reality their employer was paying them as a contractor, and reporting the money to the IRS. Several years later, massive tax bills start arriving. You see, if someone pays you to help their business, they can't deduct it on THEIR taxes unless they report it to the IRS. So, they may imply it's under the table, but paying you as a contractor is simple and easy for them to do, and they will often do it, sometimes without giving you the copy you need to file taxes. Also, contractors pay an extra 15% (roughly) in taxes, and there is no withholding to cover ANY of it!

Beware of the "Table"!

To satisfy technicality nags, if you are paid under $600, the person who paid you doesn't have to report it to the IRS, but you still have to claim it as income.

You're Doing Your Tips Wrong

No one does tips right.
Tax professionals HATE tips.

You should be keeping a record of ALL tips, both cash and credit, and reporting them to your employer every week. Your employer should be withholding taxes from your paycheck to cover those tips, and matching 7.65% as Social Security and Medicare taxes.

This explains why employers are so cavalier about this – the less tips reported by you, the less matching by them. I can't tell you what to do when rocking the boat could piss off your fellow employees, or make your boss wonder why you were hired in the first place, but I can tell you what the right thing to do is...

…and I just did.

Tax Pros are NOT All the Same

You can be a paid tax preparer. Right now. All you need is a Tax Professional ID Number and you can get that online in 5 minutes for less than $100. No training, no test, nothing. Don't believe me? Ask the IRS:

https://www.irs.gov/tax-professionals/understanding-tax-return-preparer-credentials-and-qualifications (Link #5)

Your tax guy may not even be able to represent you at an audit!

I personally think you need an Enrolled Agent or a CPA to prepare your taxes (if they have EA after their name, like, say, Kirk Taylor, EA, then they are an Enrolled Agent – or a liar). If you use a CPA, make sure they specialize in taxes like yours. CPA's know a lot more than Enrolled Agents, just not necessarily about taxes. Pick your preparer wisely – get referrals. If you don't like what's happening at the desk, don't like the results, or don't like the fees, take your papers and walk out. If the preparer isn't okay with this, and still wants you to pay, then you made the right choice by leaving.

Good preparers don't expect to be paid unless the client is 100% satisfied.

A good place to start is your parent's preparer. You can often get a really good deal from them while you are young. That said, don't ignore the advice I gave earlier about learning how taxes work.

The Tax Prep Guarantee You Get Isn't What You Think It Is

Unless you pay your Tax Dude extra, specifically for an extended guarantee, he or she probably isn't providing you the kind of guarantee you probably think you deserve. Most guarantees cover interest and penalties, not taxes. Which makes sense, since you would have owed the taxes anyway if the idiot hadn't messed them up. So, by the preparer paying the interest and penalties, you get an interest free loan from Uncle Sam.

This is, of course, little consolation when you have to come up with three grand to pay your Uncle Sam back because your Tax Genius turns out to be a Tax Dunce. I personally would only have taxes done by a SUPER Tax Genius.

They may also charge you for help in responding to the IRS, especially if you get a face to face audit. Additionally, many will try to claim that you didn't provide them the right information and documents (and they will often be right).

Oh, and that guarantee you get with your software – it's not worth squat. It is very easy for them to claim that YOU just didn't put the right information in or didn't follow the instructions correctly. As best I can tell from my experiences, it basically only covers if the programmer's messed up.

Get a Professional Tax Review Once in a While

Tax software sucks. It really does.
I'm beginning to sound like a broken record on this.

It's designed to be user friendly and easy to use. This does not result in accuracy. Odds are good that a good professional will find errors, and maybe more money.

That doesn't mean you have to pay for a review. Most pros will check your return for free, and then quote you a non-obligatory price for them to fix it. This is a win-win. Do it every three years at least (this ensures that it is not too late to get your money back).

You get peace of mind, and maybe some money.

This doesn't just apply to software. If you have been using the same tax pro for years, without really paying attention to the results, you might be getting screwed. Give a new guy (or gal) a chance to see what they can do.

This, of course, does not apply to me – I am perfect – akin to the Tax Unicorn.

If Your Tax Pro Tells You to Do Something…Do It

It shouldn't make me as happy as it does when my clients take my advice, but it does.

I spend a lot of time coming up with brilliant ideas (hence this book) and great advice, yet a noticeable minority of my clients ignore my wonderful advice. This is often to their severe detriment. Obviously, there are levels to this, but when your tax pro gets real serious, leans over the table, looks you in the eyes and gestures emphatically, it's time to pay attention. If they write something down – do it! One of my greatest skills as a tax pro is not cursing under my breath when I see that my important suggestions were blown off. This accomplishment is just below this year's goal of not asking, "What year?" when getting the birthdate of a newborn child.

Call Your Tax Guy When...

Your student loans are getting cancelled.
You start a paid internship.
You start a graduate program with a stipend.
You want to take money out of a retirement account.
You want to change your withholding.
You're going to work overseas.
Someone tells you to do something for taxes.
You're selling your rental property.
You're moving money around in investment accounts.
You're retiring.
Your income will go up a lot.
You're starting a new job.
You're starting a business.
You are going to be paid on a 1099MISC.
You're retiring.
Anything else that might change your tax situation, or you have any questions at all. People don't call (or email) their tax person often enough. That's what you pay for. If you use software...email a tax guy you trust.

Don't Call the IRS Unless…

The IRS is under-staffed and over busy. I don't have a lot of sympathy for them, but I do have sympathy for people who really need to talk to them and can't get through. This means I hate it when people call them for stupid crap that could be handled online or other ways. Here's a list of when NOT to call them:

Your refund is delayed, unless it has been AT LEAST 21 days AND you checked "Where's My Refund" at irs.gov and followed any instructions there.
Your tax return has been rejected. If you can't solve it without calling the IRS – mail your return in.
You have a non-time sensitive question and it's between January and April.
You have a generic tax question. Look it up or call a tax pro – the IRS will give you the wrong answer anyway.
You need last year's AGI or a copy of a tax return or a transcript. Sign up to get them online.

Call the IRS if:
The IRS tells you to.
"Where's My Refund" site tells you to.
You have a letter with a specific number to call.
Your tax pro tells you to.

Tax Resolution Companies Are Often Rip-offs

You know the ones I'm talking about. The ones advertised on TV or radio that say they can reduce your back taxes by thousands, get the IRS off your back, stop the garnishments, etc. I'm sure some might be good, legitimate companies, but most are little more than one trick ponies.

They'll file an Offer in Compromise (OIC), which will stop the liens and levies (as they promised). Unfortunately, the IRS doesn't approve many of these so, when they say no, the problem comes back full force, and you're out a bunch of money you paid to the tax resolution company. If you owe back taxes, talk to a local professional with good references.

More on Offers in Compromise: As a general rule, an Offer requires doubt as to whether you owe the taxes assessed, or a doubt that you will EVER have the ability to pay it back. This is a long, slow, uphill battle with a high likelihood of failure. And the resolution company will make you do most of the work you thought you were paying for.

Head of Household Doesn't Mean What You Think It Does

Well it might, but it certainly doesn't mean what it says. Head of Household essentially means Single Parent. You have to have a kid, or other qualifying dependent who lives with you at least half the year (unless they are a parent) and you have to pay at least half the cost of the place you and them live. You also can't be married as of 12/31 of the tax year, though there is an exception if you didn't spend even one night with your spouse in the last half of the year.

There are a lot of complications to this, but if you live alone and don't support a relative, you probably aren't Head of Household filing status, even if you are the Head of your Household.

If you are a single parent, unmarried, living with and supporting your own child, you are probably Head of Household. Child Support and Alimony normally have no effect on this situation.

If you are the non-custodial parent, you aren't Head of Household no matter how much Child Support you pay unless a different qualifying person lives with you.

If your situation is not obvious, check with a pro.

So when you finally graduate, get a job, and move into your own place – you are not Head of Household (until you have a kid).

There's a Tax Hit for Canceled Debt

For students, we're talking about student loans. Getting them cancelled is a total win and a happy dance is called for. Until the 1099C comes, which sometimes doesn't happen for a while, or at all - but the IRS gets it. Then a CP2000 letter appears saying you owe money on the canceled debt as if it were income.

Bummer.

The point is, if you get debt canceled, including student loans, car repossessions and foreclosures, be prepared for the 1099C, and the tax hit.

There are ways to avoid paying taxes on canceled debt, and not all student loan cancelations are taxable. The main exceptions are insolvency and if it was your principal residence, but these are complex, and you should seek professional help on them BEFORE tax time.

Pay Your Child Support, Student Loans and Taxes

You saw that I said student loans in the title, right? Deferments are okay. Payment plans are okay. Default is not.

The IRS can and will take your tax refund to pay these things and more. It's called an offset, and there's very little you can do about it. If it's your spouse's debt you can try filing an injured spouse claim to get your portion of the refund.

They won't do it on your first missed payment, but when these things go into default, they'll come get it.

Other unpaid things that will cause this are: military bonuses or pay that has to be paid back, social security or disability payments that have to be paid back, military exchange credit cards that aren't paid, and even unpaid State taxes. There are a lot of things they CAN use this for, but don't, so the list can change any day.

You can call 1-800-304-3107 to see if they are coming after your refund, though be aware that debts can be added between the time you call and getting your refund. The number covers everything EXCEPT owing the IRS for Federal taxes.

States are getting in on this act and collecting medical bills, property taxes, utility bills and all manner of other debts. One big sign that the reduced refund you got was due to debt is if the refund is not an even dollar amount.

Set Up an IRS Secure Access Account Now

The IRS (and I) are highly recommending that people get IRS Secure Access setup BEFORE they need it. Right now, you need this to easily get your tax return transcript online, which you might need to file with new software, and to get a missing ID Theft PIN. I suspect you will need it for more and more things as time passes. The process is complex, and requires a lot of information, but once done you're good. It can also take a lot of time if you don't have certain things like a cell phone in your name. It uses your credit report as one step in verifying your identity. I'm not going to go into all the details, but here's the website for more information:

https://www.irs.gov/individuals/secure-access-how-to-register-for-certain-online-self-help-tools (Link #6)

Read it, click on the "Get Transcript Online" button, and get it setup.

For students, you can't do this until after you have filed your first tax return, so you should do it before you file your second one.

Watch Out For a 1099MISC Job

Most people are employees. They get paid on a W-2, and their employer handles Social Security, Medicare and Income Tax Withholding. Your employer also matches your Social Security and Medicare taxes out of their own pocket. This is 7.65% of your income.

Because of this matching, your employer would rather you be an independent contractor paid on a 1099MISC. This makes all taxes YOUR responsibility. A lot of times, this is the right way to do things, like for real estate agents and a lot of construction workers. Sometimes it's shaky, and sometimes it's horsepucky.

You should find out, as soon as you take a job, how you're going to get paid, especially if you're in construction. If you're going to be on a 1099MISC, you should probably talk to a professional immediately to make sure you do everything the right way.

If you think you should be on a W-2, but they put you on a 1099MISC, talk to a professional about filing an SS-8 and other forms to avoid paying both halves of Social Security and Medicare.

There are a lot of college work-study programs or graduate assistant programs that pay this way. They often refer to it as a "stipend".

When you get paid by ANYBODY, you should confirm how they will report it to the IRS and what they are going to withhold. If they are paying you on a 1099MISC and not withholding, set side about 30% for taxes. This is probably overkill, but it's better than a big balance due later.

Pay Attention to State Taxes

Your tax software is probably not nearly as good at doing State taxes as it is at doing Federal taxes (and it's not that good at Federal anyway). Your tax guru might not be that good at the states that he doesn't live in either.

It can be very worthwhile to spend some time researching tax deductions and credits for your state, and reading the instruction booklet when doing your taxes. Also, if you have a state tax return done by a professional that's not working in that state, ask him about his knowledge of the state, and check things carefully. Tax pros are prickly about being questioned, and we hate admitting we don't know everything, but state taxes are one place where you need to call us on our arrogance.

In addition, if you work in a state, even if you're not a resident, you probably owe them taxes. Employers can really suck at accounting for this on your W-2. Normally if you live and work in different states, the state you live in taxes everything, the state you work in taxes the income earned in their state, and the state you live in gives you a credit for the taxes you paid to the other state so you're not double taxed. Some states have agreements with their bordering states that modify this. These are called reciprocal agreements and you probably need expert help with them because they are a bunch of legalese voodoo.

Going to school out of state does not make you a resident of that state, though often for tuition it can pay to be a resident. Handling the ins and outs of this requires a tax expert in that state, AND someone knowledgeable of college residency rules.

Also, be aware that many states have credits you can get for going to college, but they can be complicated and hard to qualify for, so knowing the rules BEFORE you go to school can be helpful.

Don't Trust Your 1098-T

The 1098-T is how a college reports how much tuition they billed you, how much was paid and how much you got in Scholarships and Grants.

Theoretically, these should be getting better this year, but they have been garbage in the past. You can get an account transcript from your school, showing what was billed and how it was paid. I highly recommend getting one and using it, vice the 1098-T.

I have a good chapter on education expenses later in this book, but here's the short version. Ignore student loans, and simply take what was billed for tuition, plus course required books and fees, and subtract money you got in scholarships, VA benefits or other financial aid that you don't have to pay back. It doesn't matter if you made up the shortfall with student loans, credit cards or cash - those were your expenses. Some credits don't let you include anything other than tuition, so make sure you know which one you're using...

Alright, I'll give more detail...American Opportunity Credit (AOC) lets you use books and fees, Lifetime Learning Credit (LLC) does not.

AOC is generally for the first four years of undergraduate school and LLC is for pretty much everything else. If you get AOC, definitely print account transcripts and save receipts for books and fees. Your preparer is required to keep copies of these, and the IRS is taking a HARD look at these. In fact, I would say AOC is more likely than anything else to get the IRS's attention on your return (short of leaving income off your return).

This was a short and sweet rundown, so you really need to read the long boring chapter on this that's coming later.

If you get GI Bill or Tuition Assistance from the military or VA, you very likely have almost no education expenses to get a credit for, even if your 1098-T says you do. The IRS is figuring this out – BEWARE!

Get Organized!

Organization is the core of success in everything you do. Taxes, College, Jobs, Life…it all hinges on knowing where your stuff is.

I know, you think you just aren't good at it. Hogwash. Organization is a skill just like everything else. It requires you to work at it, learn about it and practice it. Find out what works for you and do it!

This doesn't mean your desk and everything around it has to be perfectly organized and neat, but you should be able to find important notes and paperwork without too much trouble.

You need to write down expenses for tax information in a single, easy to find place.

You need a single to-do list that is with you wherever you go.

You need a calendar where you write down important events and due dates.

If you're an app person – use an app. If you're a software person – use software. Phone person – use your phone. Paper person – use a notebook. Organizer person – use an organizer. Whatever works for you.

The only thing that doesn't work is continuing to be disorganized and losing or forgetting important things.

Take the Freshman Prep Course

They have different names for it, but it's basically a "How to Go to College" course, often with a bunch of good life advice as well. The one at my local college is based on the "Become a Master Student" textbook. I'm not just talking about the basic, where stuff is on campus course, I'm talking about how to study, how to take tests, how to organize, etc. etc.

Pay attention in this course, since there are a lot of tools and resources that they will go over. You might be surprised at how much help is available on campus to ensure you graduate with good grades.

It's also usually an easy A.

College is Harder than High School

Some people might not find this to be true, but for most of us, college can be a culture shock. Do not assume that just because you did well in High School that you are going to coast in college.

Chances are that no one is going to remind you about upcoming quizzes and assignments. In fact, in the internet world a lot of this information might be on the course website that you are supposed to check regularly. As soon as a due date, quiz or exam date is promulgated WRITE IT DOWN!

I have a notebook for every class, and I flip to the back page and write any due dates on it as they are promulgated. I also write my course schedule on the back cover of all the notebooks.

Many instructors are going to simply put information out, without a ton of explanation or question answering. You will be expected to take notes and learn the information. Luckily, the internet has become a wonderful place for finding videos that explain things very well.

All of this is before we get to the myriad distractions that are just waiting to convince you to procrastinate on everything.

High School is Over When College Starts

Nobody cares what you were in High School. Once you get accepted into the college of your choice (or the one that would take you) virtually everything about High School ceases to matter. Grades, popularity, reputation – all meaningless. Obviously, this might not be true if you go to a local college where the majority of your classmates go, but that's still pretty unlikely.

What you do when you get to college is what is going to matter. Make a good first impression by being hard working, respectful, helpful and attentive with both the professors and your fellow students.

A good rule of thumb for any new school or job is to write off the first few months as all work – no play until you have established a good reputation with the staff and professors. This reputation will go a long way for the rest of college. Once you get settled and have figured out how to succeed, you can ease off the throttle a bit.

College is the first in a line of times where your work ethic, helpfulness, abilities and smarts are going to become more important than your popularity, what you wear and your athletic prowess. While superficial characteristics will always play a small part in how people think of you, they get less and less important as you progress into full adulthood. Many of the least "cool" kids in High School will be the most successful and popular as an adult.

LIFE IS NOT A POPULARITY CONTEST!

Figure Out What Your Teachers Want and Give it to Them

Teachers are the single most important component in determining your grade. Many of them will tell you exactly how to get a good grade. Some will come right out and say it, others will leave clues.

Find out if they value originality or adherence to form (particularly in writing). Find out if class participation matters. Find out if they grade for work or just the answers. Figure out how they give hints on testable material. Figure out any quirks or idiosyncrasies they have. Find out what pisses them off and what makes them happy. Figure out if attendance or tardiness is a big deal.

If they don't come right out and tell you what they want, pay attention for clues: writing on the board when they usually don't, deviating from a PowerPoint, change in vocal tone or manner, signs of annoyance or happiness, extra gestures, things posted on the course website. Talk to other students about what they think. Check review sites for the professor. Talk to former students.

Pay attention as the class progresses so you can adjust your assessment: if a bunch of stuff surprises you on an exam, go back and figure out if the teacher gave clues that you missed and watch for them going forward. You can also ask (see the next chapter).

One of my English teachers recently wanted a very specific academic writing form on very specific subjects. She made it clear that the structure was a key component. I struggled at first, but once I figured out what she wanted, it made it easier to get the work done and get a good grade. Many of my fellow student resisted or didn't listen and got poor grades as a result. In the end, I learned a lot more in this class than I thought I would, and this book is better for having attended that class.

Communicate with Your Teachers

Maintaining lines of communications with an instructor let them know you take the course seriously. Most professors are willing to help students who are putting in effort more than those who are not. Talking to them BEFORE things become an issue is critical. ALWAYS maintain at least the *illusion* that you care about the course beyond just getting a good grade.

Communicate with your teacher by their preferred method. Don't text or email if they say they don't want you to. Use the email address that they prefer. If you email them, give them a good subject line. Try to be clear about what you are saying. Re-read your email before sending. If the email is complex, consider asking someone else to read it before you send it to make sure it says what you think it does.

If you are unsure about something, ask them. Be respectful and NEVER be confrontational. Respect their time by being prepared when you communicate. Ask your question in a clear, well thought out manner. Consider writing some notes before an appointment with the instructor to make sure you have an effective conference.

If you are struggling, ask for help early, but make sure you do your best to analyze the SPECIFICS of what is giving you trouble. "I just don't get it" are the most hated words from a student. WHAT are you struggling with? WHEN did you start getting lost?

If you get a bad grade on an assignment, especially one that doesn't have clear cut grading, don't ask "Why did I do bad?" instead ask, "What can I do to get a better grade next time?" Don't grade grope!

Take Notes

Thus, begin the chapters in which I nag you...

Have a notebook for each of your classes. Track required tasks by date in the back and take notes from the front.

You are already IN class, so it's not like you are going to be doing anything else useful. Take advantage of the time and write down important information from the class. If your professor emphasizes something – write it down. If it's implied that it might be on the test – write it down. If a problem gets worked on the board – write it down. Listening, reading, writing and reviewing are all different ways to commit things to memory. By taking notes, you are accomplishing two of the four and already beginning the process of converting things from short term to long term memory.

Review your notes within 24 hours of the conclusion of a class.

Even if you could pass the class in your sleep, taking notes develops good habits that will help you with the courses you are going to struggle with. In addition, teachers notice students who are taking notes, and are more likely to give them the benefit of the doubt if they run into trouble.

Put Your Phone Away During Class!

Have some respect.

Don't text.
Don't surf the internet.
Don't check your messages.

DON'T DO IT!!!

Put it away, with the volume off, and check things on your break.

I shouldn't need to explain why.

Study!!!

Seriously…you need to study.

The process of taking notes is half of the process of committing things to memory. Review the notes within 24 hours. This is critical to mastering the material.

After you've done the above things, make a plan for continuing to review old material as you process new information. If you are strong in an area, you may only need to do the 24-hour review and a final pre-exam review. For more complicated information, you may need to review daily. Even a half hour of review can make a huge difference.

Don't let ANYTHING sit for more than three days without at least a quick review. Memory and skills stagnate quickly. You will spend WAY less time reviewing regularly than you will cramming at the last minute to get the same level of mastery.

Every teacher I ever had is going to hate the next paragraph…sorry guys:

Cramming is not a great method to rely on, but is still a component of a good study plan. When conducting routine studying, identify areas of memorization or weakness that you can benefit from last minute studying. Highlight these areas and review them just before bed on the day before the exam and in the last few minutes before exam time.

Don't Procrastinate!

It took me a month to write this sentence because I just kept finding better things to do.

I think my windows are dirty…I'll be right back…
.
.
.

You're still here? Crap. I really need to get this thing written.

Procrastination is a psychological process whereby we choose to prioritize lower importance things due to a desire not to do a higher priority project. Like writing a stupid chapter about procrastination.

Try writing a schedule where you allocate time to various priorities such that you accomplish small parts each day.

That's a great idea. I'm going to write a schedule for writing this page. Hang on…
.
.
.

Okay, I am scheduled to write 3 lines before lunch.
Lunch.
Should I eat at home or go out?

DONE! Hell, this is easy. I'll be back after dinner for the next three lines.
.
.
.

Procrastination is a waste of time (this plus the 2 extra lines I wrote before lunch mean I'm good.)

Seriously – figure this crap out and stay focused.

Learn Teamwork

At some point, you are going to be assigned a group project or be asked to work in a group in class. Being able to work effectively with others will be a key skill (as will how to deal with incompetent, lazy losers who won't pull their weight). Even when not assigned to a group, working with your fellow students can be extremely helpful in ensuring you get good scores.

I'm no expert in this area. In fact, I have a T-shirt that says, "Teamwork is a lot of people doing what I say." This was a thoroughly successful system when I was a Master Chief in the Navy, but slightly less effective now. The key is to pay attention to group dynamics, and assign roles based on the skills and preferences of the group members. Holding each other accountable is critical, but doing so without sounding like a whiney b-word is harder.

The freshman skills class I mentioned earlier usually provides some good advice on this subject.

I guess I'll give you my best thoughts and leave it at that. Leave the petty BS behind. Do your part on time or early. NEVER make people wait on you. Minimize distractions and stay focused when in a group setting. Be respectful. Learn to like your co-workers. Write down assignments, tasks, due dates and ideas and share copies around. If things just aren't working, communicate with your professor for help.

Understand How to Take Exams

Taking tests is a skill that most people just kind of absorb over the years, but thinking about it and changing methods can make a big difference.

Some of the difference is in preparation. Multiple choice exams require you to recognize an answer rather than knowing it cold. This means you can focus on key words rather than solid memorization. Essay tests require you to understand the material much more deeply, and often require you to have original thoughts on the subject. Planning your "original" thoughts in advance can make a big difference. Short answer and definition type tests are better studied for by focusing on the series of words that make the definition work, rather than memorizing every word.

How you take a test also depends on the type of test it is. The more information you get beforehand the better. What kind of questions, how many, how are they weighted, is time a big factor, is it heavy on calculations or memorization, how will it be graded, is there a penalty for guessing, how much partial credit for work, etc, etc. This information can be gotten from the instructor, former students, the course web page and even sometimes on the internet. Finding details of what TYPE of questions are on a test is not cheating as opposed to finding out the exact questions or answers.

The two most important things to note are time required and guessing penalty. If the test is going to be tight on time, have a plan to get the most points fastest. Prioritize the questions that you can get completely right, sorted by how fast you can get points adding up. Ten 2-point questions that you can do in 5 minutes are better than one 20-point question that will take 15 minutes. If there is no penalty for guessing, answer every question, especially multiple choice and true/false types. If time is a factor, answer all questions (except maybe ones you have no chance of getting points) before checking your work or answers.

If time isn't a factor, work the test with the stuff you are good at, or are likely to forget, first, and then go back to work on the other stuff.

Make a note somehow for questions you really think you need to go back and look at. When double checking, use a check mark to indicate questions you have checked. If there are two ways to do a problem, work it both ways until you are sure of the answer.

Never change an answer unless you are pretty sure it's wrong. Generally, your first instinct will be right.

Read every question carefully. Note the information they are looking for, and organize given information. This is a critical thing to double check when verifying your answers.

For multiple choice questions, try to eliminate answers that are obviously wrong and then pick one that is right. For long multiple-choice exams, if you guess, try to use a random method like the second hand of a clock to avoid patterns.

For essay type questions, be organized and focus on the information asked. If you have no clue, try to spit out as many key words and phrases as you can, organized with a bit of good sounding word salad. Who knows, you might pick up a point or two.

Don't grade yourself or get discouraged, ESPECIALLY while still taking the exam. Relax. Take Deep Slow Breaths.

Get a good night's sleep. Get to the exam early. Have a decent breakfast. Caffeinate early if that's your thing. Do a little light, no pressure cramming once you get to the exam site.

Consider Community College

Too few people consider Community College or Technical School as an option. Obviously, if you know what you want to study, are motivated, and your parents are comfortably paying for school (or some other thing other than loans is covering it) then go for the school and program you want. Otherwise, here are some reasons to consider Community College:

If you don't know for sure what you want to study or aren't absolutely sure you won't change your mind, go to Community College for a lot less money, taking solid courses that will transfer to a variety of degrees, and figure out what you like and don't like.

If you have to take a lot of loans out for school or your parents are stretching to pay for your school, go to Community College for a FRACTION of what regular colleges cost. In most states it's practically free. You would be crazy to pay a fortune for two years of college that you can get much cheaper at Community College.

If you're not that confident academically, go to Community College as a good place to get used to the college class environment without all the distractions of a major college. It's also a low risk endeavor. If you aren't going to finish college, better not to have paid a fortune for the degree you don't have.

If you don't have the grades to get into the best schools, going to Community College and doing well often makes it a lot easier to get into a good 4-year school. This is especially true for schools in the same state.

If you're not sure about not living at home, there is almost certainly a Community College near your parent's house that you can commute to. In addition to not having to deal with crazy roommates, you don't have to pay for room and board, which lowers the overall cost of college even more. In addition, there are a lot fewer distractions (like parties) at home then at college.

Don't listen to people who look down on Community College. Those people are elitist idiots. If you go to Community College for 2 years, and then finish at a prestigious 4-year school, your degree will look exactly the same as someone who paid twice as much as you for the same degree.

Not listening to people spewing crap ideas and suggestions is a skill that will pay off all your life.

To be clear, we are not referring to the totally NOT crap ideas I am spewing in this book.

Power Your Way Through School

Don't Give Up.

Really. Get help, get to work, and knock that stuff out. College can be paradise or it can suck ass. Either way, getting your degree finished is almost universally good for your life.

Some days you are going to wish you never went to college. Other days you are going to love every class. Focus on the good days, and let the bad days slide away.

I can personally attest to the fact that getting it done in one shot is the easiest, cheapest and most certain way of getting your degree.

There are numerous resources available to help you if you are struggling: family, friends, administration, teachers, and fellow students. Seek them out and ask for help. Chances are that even the people who look like they are coasting through school could use a bit of motivation. Team up and help each other out.

Be Careful with Student Loans

I'm sure the underwater basket weaving degree sounded good at the time, but it's doubtful you'll be paying back the student loan with the wages earned from it.

A degree is an investment. If the returns on the investment aren't high enough compared to the costs, then it's a bad investment. If you borrow to make the investment, you have to be doubly careful.

Student loans are extremely difficult to get discharged short of paying them. Deferments just delay the inevitable and Income Based Repayment is not all it's cracked up to be, especially if you end up married.

I would argue that if you aren't in an extremely lucrative degree program, with a high likelihood of graduation and employment, student loans should be kept to the absolute minimum – often this means state schools and community college. Borrowing to cover living expenses is a terrible idea. Borrowing more than is needed for the degree is crazy.

Even lawyers are learning that paying off their student loans is extremely difficult, and these people are supposed to be the smart ones!

Every week we hear breathless warnings about the student debt crisis we are facing, yet this doesn't seem to deter students from taking on more debt. Don't follow the herd!

As far as taxes go, you can deduct up to $2500 in student loan interest per return, subject to an income limitation. For most people this will be no more than $550 on their taxes, and for many people it will be less than $250.

Your Parents Aren't Obligated to Pay for Your School

One of the things people need to learn about money is that anything spent on one thing is unavailable for another. I compare potential expenditures with what vacation I would have to sacrifice in order to pay for it. Seriously, I love to travel. Obviously, the $10,000 kitchen renovation keeps getting postponed. Singapore, here we come!

If your parents are paying for your college you should be grateful. Think about what your parents could do if they weren't paying for your school. A car? A home addition? Retirement? Travel? They don't HAVE to sacrifice these things so you can go to school.

I don't write this to shame you, but to remind you that, unless your parents are very well off, you should take the sacrifice they made into account when making decisions:

1. Make good choices about college, taking cost into account. If your parents aren't wealthy, consider Community College. Consider the cost of in-state versus out of state and whether staying at home would be practical.

2. Complete your education efficiently. If you aren't sure what you want to be, focus on classes that apply to a wide variety of degrees. Avoid wasteful electives. Take the maximum class load you can successfully complete.

3. Put real effort into school and pass your courses and finish your degree. Sacrificing a big purchase for your kid's degree turns into a horrendous kick in the unmentionables when they don't even manage to finish.

Also, consider thanking them.

About Scholarships and Grants

As a general rule, scholarships and grants that are paid and used for tuition and most course related fees and expenses are tax free. If scholarships and grants exceed these amounts, the excess is generally taxable income.

To simplify, you add up qualified expenses (no matter how paid) and compare them to scholarships and grants and pay taxes on the excess or get a potential credit if it is less than expenses. Room and board, travel, clerical help, research and equipment not directly required by the course don't qualify as expenses.

This is complicated and may require professional help if you have unusual situations or expenses.

All the above said, try and get your college, room and board, and other expenses paid with scholarships and grants. Paying taxes on free money is a total win.

There's a later chapter that covers the tax implications of too many scholarships or grants.

Colleges are Businesses…

And their goal is generally to make a profit. This often applies to "public" universities and colleges as well.

They have slick sales pitches and pretty brochures touting all the wonderful things they do for you. They have lots of extras you can pay for. They want your money.

I'm not saying they are a bunch of shyster crooks (nor am I saying they aren't), but what I am saying is not to take everything they say at face value. One look at your college textbook prices, and the way some colleges work hard to prevent you from buying them from someone else, like access codes needed for online stuff as an example, will remind you that they are after your money.

Be skeptical. Ask around about your options. Don't assume that just because a college employee tells you something that it has to be true.

Pay Attention to the Marketability of Your Degree

I know I briefly covered this before, but I wanted to expand upon it.

I'm not suggesting that it only makes sense to get a degree that is guaranteed to make you a ton of money. What I am suggesting is that you need to have a plan to pay for your degree, especially if you are using debt to fund it. The amount of money your degree can be expected to make is a key component of this.

Under no circumstances should you use your college's information on degree marketability. Nor should you use your peers. Use a reputable, independent source. CNN, Forbes, Money and Kiplinger's often do articles on the subject and these are good sources. Talking to people in the specific industry your degree applies to is really helpful, especially if you can get your foot in the door for a prospective job in the process.

Make sure to pay attention to what jobs are available, what they pay TO START, how much advancement there is, and WHERE the jobs are. A 6-figure salary only works if you are willing to go where the job is.

Don't just assume that the "usual" great jobs are that great. Lawyers with expensive degrees are struggling, and doctor marketability varies greatly with the specialty.

Track Your College Expenses

If you are going to take advantage of the tax credits available (or your parents are) you need to accurately track what you spent on your college. This includes amounts spent on books, supplies and equipment.

The easiest way to track expenses is in a notebook you use specifically for this purpose. Anytime you pay something, write it down and save the receipt. You should also write down sources of college funds as they are used EXCEPT LOANS. We do not care about loans, they count just like you used cash.

Categorize in such a way that you can break down the expenses and payment amounts into the following categories:

    a. Total tuition charged
    b. Total necessary books and fees. "Necessary" means things like a computer that is needed for college, and also tools and equipment for practical types of education. They can't be general study supplies, athletic fees and other things unless they are needed for a specific course of study. When in doubt, write it down and let your tax pro sort it out, but be specific enough for them to know what it was for.
    c. Total charges for room and board
    d. Total amount of scholarships and grants
    e. Total Savings Bonds sold during the year and how much of that was interest.
    f. Total amount withdrawn from tax advantaged education accounts – meaning 529 plans or Education Savings Accounts.

I know this sounds like a lot of work, but it will make life easier come tax time and ensure you get everything you are entitled to.

College Tax Benefits

This section is long, complicated, and copied in large part out of my book Everyday Taxes:

This is a HUGE section with lots of possibilities, so I'm going to try to break it down as much as possible. Start reading with the very first part and then stop when you have your situation covered. Make sure that you don't use the same expenses for more than one credit or deduction. That's a serious no-no.

1. Determine who you can claim expenses for:

You can claim education expenses and credits for yourself and your spouse if you are Married Filing Jointly. You can also claim them for someone who you claim as a dependent on your tax return. You can claim the credits for a dependent even if they pay the expenses themselves. For students reading this book, it means if your parent's claim you as a dependent, they get the credit...PERIOD.

2. Gather your information and documents:

The school is going to (or should) send you a Form 1098-T that details what they think you paid. Starting in 2017, you MUST have a 1098-T to claim the American Opportunity Credit. This form is useful for a lot of things, but don't rely on it solely to determine what you paid. Verify that it matches what you think you paid, and you should get an account transcript from the school showing what was charged, what was paid, and how it was paid. The one nice thing about the 1098-T is that it will tell you if you were more than half-time, if you were a graduate student, and it has the data needed to fill out your tax forms. Using the 1098-T, your payment receipts and other documentation, get the following information:
      a. Total tuition charged
      b. Total course-related books and fees.
      c. Total charges for room and board
      d. Total amount of scholarships and grants
      e. Status of at least half-time (from 1098-T)

  f. Year of college as determined by the school (freshman, sophomore, junior, senior or graduate as of the beginning of the tax year)

  g. Whether you have ever been convicted of a felony drug offense

  h. Total amount of U.S. Savings Bond interest used to pay for college

  i. Total amount of money from tax advantaged tuition plans, such as Coverdell Educational Savings Accounts, Qualified Tuition Plans, Prepaid College Plans, 529 plans or other state-sponsored plans used for education

You'll notice we don't talk about student loans because the expenses are considered paid even if you use student loans or a credit card.

3. Determine if college expenses exceed scholarships and tax advantaged plan sources:

Take the total of a and b from above (your college expenses), and compare it to the total of d, h and i (your tax advantaged funding sources and scholarships). If your expenses exceed your tax advantaged funding sources and scholarships, you have the potential for a credit or deduction. Keep reading. If they do not, then you have a problem. You need to see if you have taxable income from scholarships. This will be discussed in Step 7 and later.

4. See if you can use the American Opportunity Credit (AOC):

This is the best credit available because you get up to $2,500 of credit, with $1,000 refundable on only $4,000 of expenses. Refundable means you get it even after your tax is reduced to zero. Generally, you should always shoot for this one. I'm going to refer to the letters from 2, above, to move things along when available. This credit is the one that will come up if you are attending a standard two or four-year college with the intention of getting a degree or other certificate. You get it for the first four years of education - freshman, sophomore, junior, senior, as determined by the college, even if it takes you more than four years to progress through them. In a confusing twist, however, each student gets a maximum of 4 tax-

years' worth of AOC in their life. For the normal student, they will have 4 years of schooling spanning 5 tax years. Most students begin college in Fall of the same year they graduate high school; half of their college senior year will be in the spring of their fourth year—the fifth tax year of college. This means that you can take the AOC for any four of those five years. If you take 6 years to graduate, you still get any four of those six years. Many tax professionals will spend a lot of time trying to anticipate the best four years to take. My recommendation is to take it the first four years the credit is available—you never know what's going to happen in the future. The only caveat is that if you only have a couple hundred dollars of expenses in the first year, you might want to wait to start taking the credit the following tax year. Otherwise, you won't get much out of the AOC and one of your 4 years is wasted.

One other point: you can take as many AOCs as you have students on your tax return. If you, your wife and your three children all qualify, you can get FIVE separate AOCs. Here are the rules once you've figured out that the year qualifies:

    a. If college expenses determined in 3 (above) do not exceed scholarships and tax advantaged sources, you get nothing.

    b. If the answer to 2e is not at least half-time, you cannot get AOC.

    c. If you have been convicted of a felony drug offense, you don't get AOC.

    d. You have to be attending an eligible school with the intention of getting a degree or other recognized educational credential, which includes virtually every accredited postsecondary institution. This can even include colleges outside the U.S. if they are eligible to participate in the U.S. Federal Student Aid program. The college can tell you if they are eligible.

    e. You cannot be filing Married Filing Separately.

    f. If your AGI exceeds $180,000 (MFJ) or $90,000 (HH or Single) you cannot get AOC.

    g. If your AGI exceeds $160,000 (MFJ) or $80,000 (HH or Single) your credit will be limited. In this case, you should figure out the AOC, the Lifetime Learning Credit (LLC, next) and the Tuition and Fees Deduction (after LLC) to see which gets you the most money. If it is very close, save the AOC for a later year, since you only get 4 years of AOC, unless this is your final year as an undergraduate.

    h. Calculate your expenses for Form 8863. This number will be a + b - d - h - i which is tuition plus course-related fees, minus scholarships, grants and tax advantaged funding sources. This is the number you will use when filling out Form 8863 or entering data in your software program, though software may ask for a, b, d, h and i through separate questions.

5. If you don't get AOC, see if you can get the Lifetime Learning Credit (LLC):

The LLC is a nice credit, but not as lucrative as the AOC. You get 20% of eligible expenses, up to $2,000 of credit. The expenses are more limited, but the rules for qualifying are less restrictive. This is the credit you would use if you had already used 4 years of AOC, weren't attending half-time, weren't in a degree or credential program, were a graduate student, or already had a four-year degree. Another major difference is that while you can get an AOC for as many students as appear on the tax return, you can get a maximum of $2,000 of LLC, per tax return, regardless of how many students are on the tax return. Here's how we work the LLC:

    a. If college expenses determined in 3 (above) do not exceed scholarships and tax advantaged sources, you get nothing.

    b. If the answer to 2e is not at least half-time, you can still get LLC.

    c. If you have been convicted of a felony drug offense, you don't get LLC.

    d. You have to be attending an eligible school, with or without the intention of getting a degree or credential, which includes virtually every accredited postsecondary institution. This can even include colleges outside the U.S. if they are eligible to participate in the U.S. Federal Student Aid program. The college can tell you if they are eligible. This includes truck driving school, welding school and other non-degree attaining schools.

    e. You cannot be filing Married Filing Separately.

    f. If your AGI exceeds $136,000 (MFJ) or $68,000 (HH or Single) you cannot get LLC.

g. If your AGI exceeds $116,000 (MFJ) or $58,000 (HH or Single) your credit will be limited, you should check to see if the Tuition and Fees deduction will provide you with more benefit.

h. Calculate your expenses for Form 8863. This number will be a - d - h - i this is tuition without course-related fees, minus scholarships, grants and tax advantaged funding sources. This is the number you will use when filling out Form 8863 or entering data in your software program, though software may ask for a, d, h and i through separate questions.

6. If you don't get AOC or LLC, see if the Tuition and Fees Deduction will benefit you:

This deduction was eliminated for 2018 and later years, but I'm leaving it in because they LOVE reinstating it at the last possible second. For 2017, it was reinstated on February 8th of 2018 – AFTER the tax filing season had started for 2017.

The tuition and fees deduction is the least beneficial of the education benefits; you get a deduction from income instead of a tax credit. It is an "above the line" deduction, which means it improves your taxes whether you itemize or not and may reduce your AGI for figuring other limitations. The expenses that you can deduct for this deduction are virtually the same as the AOC, except that books and course-related fees are only included if they MUST be paid directly to the education institution as a condition of enrollment. One big caveat on all this education stuff is that the AOC and the LLC have no effect on state taxes. This deduction often does, so when determining whether this is better than the LLC or AOC, make sure to check your state taxes as well. Here are the details:

a. If college expenses determined in 3 (above) do not exceed scholarships and tax advantaged sources, you get nothing.

b. If the answer to 2e is not at least half-time, you can still get this deduction.

c. If you have been convicted of a felony drug offense, you still get this deduction.

d. You have to be attending an eligible school with or without the intention of getting a degree or credential, which includes virtually every accredited postsecondary institution. This can even include colleges outside the U.S. if they are eligible to participate in the U.S. Federal Student Aid program. The college can tell you if they are eligible. This includes truck driving school, welding school and other non-degree attaining schools.

    e. You cannot be filing Married Filing separately.

    f. If your AGI exceeds $160,000 (MFJ) or $80,000 (HH or Single) you cannot get this deduction.

    g. You can deduct a maximum of $4,000 if your income is less than $130,000 (MFJ) or $65,000 (Single or HH). If your income is between $130,000 and $160,000 (MFJ) or between $65,000 and $80,000 (HH or Single) you can deduct $2,000. This is per tax return, not per person.

    h. Calculate your expenses for Form 8917. This number will be a + b (if required to be paid to the institution as discussed above) - d - h - i (tuition with required course-related fees minus scholarships, grants and tax advantaged funding sources). This is the number you will use when filling out Form 8917 or entering data in your software program, though software may ask for a, b, d, h and i through separate questions.

7. If you have QTPs, ESAs, 529s, or other tax advantaged education savings, account for them:

Bottom line, do not withdraw more from these accounts than your educational expenses. These are tuition, fees, and room and board (does not have to be paid through the college but cannot exceed what the college would have charged). Make sure you are enrolled at least half-time. Lastly, make sure you don't include expenses paid with these funds when calculating any of the credits or deductions above.

8. If you use Savings Bond proceeds to pay for education, figure out what's tax free:

When you cash in U.S. Savings Bonds, you normally pay federal tax on the interest, the difference between what you paid for the bond and how much they pay you when cashing in, but no state tax. When you use it for education, however, you can exclude the interest from income. That said, it's actually one of the more complicated subjects with regard to education expenses, because the exclusion is limited by how much cash you get, and not just by the interest you received. I would suggest talking to a tax professional before cashing in bonds for education, but here are a few simple tips to keep you out of trouble:

    a. Make sure your AGI is below $121,600 (MFJ) or $81,100 (Single or HH) before you cash in savings bonds for education. Above this income your deduction starts phasing out (Completely gone at $151,600 (MFJ) and $96,100 (Single or HH.)

    b. Make sure that you don't cash in more in bonds (not just the interest) than the tuition you have to pay, less any other scholarships or tax advantaged education savings you are using. Room and Board does not count.

    If you follow these rules, you should be safe.

9. If you get more in scholarships and grants than tuition, prepare to pay taxes on it:

Did that scare you? Good. Now we can determine if you need to pay taxes on it, but, before that, let me say one thing. If you can find a way to get scholarships and grants that exceed the cost of your tuition, you win. Seriously. You will have to pay taxes on the excess (maybe), but it's free money! Pay the taxes and be happy! First, take the amount from 2d (scholarships and grants) and subtract a and b from it. If the number is positive, it's taxable, and you add it to line 7 of Form 1040 (the same line as your wages from your W-2s). If the number is negative, you do not need to include anything as income.

I want to add that college savings plans and scholarships interact in weird ways, so if you have both, talk to a tax professional BEFORE withdrawing from the 529.

10. VA benefits. If you use VA benefits or the GI Bill to pay for school, none of the benefits are taxable, including any housing allowances you get, however, you can't get deductions or credits for expenses paid by the VA or with VA money. The benefits can interact weirdly with the credits and deductions, so I would check with an expert before filing.

Do an Internship

If you get offered an internship, paid or unpaid, try to do it. These are great ways to gain skills, get connections, get a job and figure out if you are going to hate your chosen career.

If you have options, be choosy about which ones to take. Some are essentially gopher slavery, where you learn nothing, get treated like a peon and don't get paid. This might still be a good option if it has a history of leading to good employment. Many internships are literally a combination of on-the-job training and job interview, where the employer figures out if they want to hire you when you graduate.

Either way, bust your tail as an intern. Be the best intern they have ever had. It cannot hurt you to develop a reputation as a go-getter. At the very least, it will give you a credible reference who isn't a friend or teacher.

A Little Section on the Military

First of all, if the military is paying for your college through Tuition Assistance, you probably are entitled to very little tax credit. You don't get the credit for things paid by the military. If the Veterans Administration is paying for your college through the GI Bill, you almost certainly aren't entitled to any tax credit.

The military is an extremely under-appreciated option for most young people. If you do one hitch, your bachelor's degree is essentially paid for by the GI Bill, and they pay you tax-free to attend college after you get out. If you take advantage of college opportunities while on active duty, the GI Bill can be used for a Master's or Doctorate degree, or for your spouse or children.

Retiring from the military has a ton of advantages, not the least of which are a lifetime pension and health care.

Don't be afraid to check them out.

FYI – recruiters lie.

More About Life and Finances

The remaining chapters are about life and finances, an area where I am extremely experienced, but not a qualified expert. I just thought that a book for students would be wasted if I didn't throw in my two cents on how to live and be happy.

Read on, and take what you want from it.

Have an Emergency Fund

This is probably the best piece of advice that nobody follows. Having some cash tucked away makes a broken-down car, emergency travel, job loss or other unexpected expenses a problem, but not a catastrophe. A good tax refund is a nice way to start one.

Your emergency fund should be 3 to 6 months of living expenses.

The cool thing about having an emergency fund, is that this dude named Murphy, who has a law named after him, keeps track of who does and who doesn't have an emergency fund. Emergencies happen to people without an emergency fund, and generally don't happen to people who are prepared to handle them.

You should also have a budget, preferably one that has a budget item that puts money into your emergency fund at a rate that would refill it in 36 months or less. If it gets overfunded you can shift the money to something fun, but budgets keep your money under control, help avoid excess debt accumulation and let you plan for the future.

While I was writing this book, the government was in the middle of a shutdown over a border wall. Government shutdowns have become routine enough that my sympathy for government employees who don't have an emergency fund has gotten a lot lower. An emergency fund is not just a good idea, it is ESSENTIAL!

Start Saving Now

This is less about a specific plan or goal, and more about developing a habit. Being able to save will help you in a myriad of ways in your future life. Start by saving for small goals, like your next TV or a newer car. Then build up to saving for retirement, a house, vacations, new cars etc. Everything that you might use a credit card to buy is something you should save for instead. It takes longer to get some things, but you end up paying a lot less for them.

These are the things I have a savings fund for:

Long Term Emergency Fund (new roof type thing)
Short Term Emergency Fund (broken appliance type thing)
Vacation
Car Repairs
New Car
VIP tickets to an annual celebrity golf tournament
Vacation Home Annual Fees (NOT a timeshare – a family home)
Christmas and Birthday Gifts
Vacation Home Addition

I used to have a fund for retirement, but it's now fully funded – and I am already semi-retired. I also used to have a lot of categories for furniture, remodels and other things, but I overfund my emergency fund so much that they generally end up having extra money in them for those things. I don't save for a house because mine is paid for now.

You can set up your savings based on your life and what you expect to need. Mine are obviously different than a lot of people's because of the stage in life I am in and my weird career situation.

Invest in Tax Sheltered Accounts

There are very few sure-fire ways to save money on taxes. This is one of them. I'm talking about 401k's, IRA's, 457's, SIMPLE's, 403b's, SEP's and all the other fancy account types out there. Many of them can be done right through your job, and come right out of your paycheck. I'll let your financial guy (NOT a banker) help you navigate which one and why, but all of them save you money on taxes, either now or in the future. Put as much in them as you can afford. The only specific advice I will give is that if your employer has a match to your contributions, invest enough to get the match before you do any other investing. Free money beats everything.

As a general rule, the younger you are, the more you should focus on Roth type accounts, but you really should talk to a financial advisor and not just your tax person.

When I said earlier not to do something just for the tax benefit, this is the time to ignore that advice. Talk to your financial advisor AND your tax dude to figure out the right TYPE of retirement account to invest in, and what investments to focus on – but invest in them for sure!

Every time you get a raise, your investments get a raise! This is most easily accomplished by bumping your 401k, or similar account percentage up when you get a raise, such that your paycheck still increases, but so does your savings rate.

Avoid Over-Complicated Investments

If investing was simple, you wouldn't need an investment advisor. So how complicated do you think an investment advisor can make things in order to justify their fees. This is not a slam on investment advisors in general, but on the unscrupulous ones. If your advisor can't or won't explain an investment until you FULLY understand it, then they might not be a great fit.

There are a ton of investment options out there that are simple and easy to understand. Index Funds are a perfect example, where you pool your money with a million other investors and buy every stock in a given index. The Dow is an example of an index, with just 30 stocks in it, and the S&P 500 is another example. It has the 500 biggest stocks in America in it. There are also Lifecycle funds where you invest based on your expected retirement year, and the fund automatically adjusts.

I'm not suggesting you don't need an advisor (or that you do). What I am saying is that you need to understand your investments, and that over-complicated investments are a warning sign.

Decide how much research and learning you want to do, and then decide how you want to invest based on that. I can recommend the books Personal Finance for Dummies and Investing for Dummies as a starting point.

SCAMS!!!!

There are a million, and they're easy to avoid. If someone calls saying you owe them money, it's probably a scam (unless you actually owe them money – which you should already know).

1. The IRS isn't coming to arrest you.
2. Timeshares are generally a scam.
3. Most investment "opportunities" are a scam (you should find your investment advisor, not the other way around).
4. There is no money that needs your help to get into the country.
5. You don't have to pay anything up front if you win the lottery.
6. Don't click on unknown email links.
7. Always be suspicious of emails from financial institutions.
8. When in doubt, go directly to a website (typing the address in the browser window) vice using a link.
9. Phone calls and door-to-door sellers are often scams. Be VERY careful if they involve automatic payments or extended contracts.
10. NEVER give out personal information over the phone or via email unless YOU initiated the transaction.
11. Dating sites are full of scams (never send compromising photos – NEVER)
12. Check out any charity you are thinking of donating to by using an independent review site.
13. E-mails asserting they have compromising information on you are scams. Often, they will have an old password of yours and will claim they got it from a porn site you were browsing and will threaten to expose the porn you watched. They actually got your password off a list from an old website hack. Think about it, if they installed a key-logger on your computer, they could empty your bank account without extorting you.
14. Your family member is not stranded in another country.
15. Don't click on "lost package" links from Fedex, UPS, etc. If you check the email address it won't be Fedex.com. If you are unsure, go to their website directly and check.
16. If you are selling something, don't accept a check for more than the amount where you wire transfer the difference.
17. Microsoft doesn't need to fix your computer.

Life Insurance

Eventually, someone will be relying on you for income or support. When that happens, you will need life insurance. This chapter is not to nag you to get it (though you should). This chapter is telling you to get Term Insurance.

Period.

If it's not plain old vanilla term life insurance, it's probably a rip-off. If it has names like Universal, Variable, Whole or any combination of those, it is a rip-off. Salesman are great at making these "investment" type life insurance policies sound awesome, but they're not. The salesman probably believes it, because he was taught everything about it by his bosses.

Don't do it.

Everyone I know who got these types of insurance regretted it. Every reputable investment advice show I've listened to says stick with term.

Term Life Insurance. Period.

The only acceptable add on type words are 20-year level or some such. This means the premiums are fixed for a certain number of years.

Trust me on this one.

Renter's Insurance

When you rent, you need renter's insurance.

Your landlord's insurance doesn't cover any of your stuff.

Renter's Insurance is one or two hundred dollars a year and is worth every penny.

Beware of Credit

I have a rule. Credit is for things you NEED, cash is for things you want. Telling the difference is the hard part. Credit is like agreeing to pay $1000 for something worth $700. Even 0% credit isn't all it's cracked up to be.

It is very easy to get into trouble with credit. Be different. Be unique. Don't be like everybody else getting into debt until it strangles your budget. Resolve to not use debt unless absolutely necessary. Do finances right and this will pretty much be your house only.

So, what's a need?

Let me give some examples: You might need a car to get to work. You don't need a $10,000 car. You need a $3,000 car. You WANT the more expensive car. Pay cash for the $10,000 car or finance the $3,000 car (if you have to). You need a bed. You don't need a nice frame and an expensive mattress. If you can't afford to pay cash for it, get a cheap mattress and box spring (or an air mattress). You need food. You don't need restaurant food or expensive ingredients.

See how that works for you. I cannot over emphasize how much avoiding debt will make your life easier.

Be Nice!

Now we begin the chapters where I nag you like I was your own Mother!

The world has plenty of jerks.
Don't be one of them.
We need more nice people.

A lot of people will tell you that it's easy to be nice to people, but it's not really. We are surrounded by people and media yelling at each other and insulting each other. Harmless banter is very often made up of insults. Surrounded by all this, it can be hard to remember to treat people nicely.

Being nice is a habit. You have to work at it. Lobbing a funny insult can be satisfying, and often harmless, but be careful of doing it about the same thing, with the same person. Also, don't assume that just because you wouldn't be bothered by it that someone else won't. People have a lot of stuff going on in their heads, and many people are very insecure. When in doubt, say something nice.

It's not just about talk. Help people out. Actions speak louder than words, and giving someone a helping hand is enormously satisfying.

Strive to leave the world better than you found it through your own PERSONAL actions.

Eat Right. Don't Drink Too Much. Sleep

Life is good when you're young. Many of you can eat what you want, stay up all night drinking, and be ready to go in the morning and not put a single pound on.

This is not going to last…

Either way, you will perform better if you do things in moderation. Tests are easier when you are well rested and your blood sugar is in a nice balance.

I'm not the guy to get into specifics on this. If a friend saw me in a gym he would have to ask if they had started serving beer. Even so, pay attention to the following:

1. Eat mostly good foods and eat them in moderation.
2. Drink a good amount of water and limit how much bad drinks you drink.
3. Be careful with what drugs you take (legal and illegal).
4. Try to get a good night's sleep, every night, at around the same times.
5. Try to exercise every day, at least a little.

You would be surprised how good you feel when you take care of yourself.

Don't Lock In your Political Opinions

I have no objection to you being politically active. I would, in fact, encourage it.

Just be aware that your opinions will change as you age. You will gain more experience, more knowledge and interact with more people directly affected by political programs and ideas.

This is a good thing.

Be careful slinging insults and labels at people you disagree with. Don't assume that you know WHY someone voted or acted the way they did.

I'm a really smart person. I'm pretty well informed.
I've been wrong about a whole lot of things.
I am probably wrong about many things now, though hopefully nothing in this book.

It can be very humbling to discover that something you held very dear as an absolute truth turns out to be more nuanced than you thought. Or worse, you find out it's complete bunk. It's a bit easier if you weren't a complete jerk about it for years.

I said earlier to be nice.
This applies to politics as well.

On Getting Married...

Now I'm really going to nag!

I was a Navy Master Chief as the culmination of 25 years in the Navy. Part of my job was to keep my sailors from doing stupid stuff with their lives. Things like marrying the stripper they just met. I'm not even joking.

I developed some pretty hard and fast (also unenforceable) rules that I used to advise my charges. They were based on experience, studies and statistics. They don't apply to everyone, but the problem is that everyone thinks THEY are the one they don't apply to. THEY are usually wrong.

Before you marry:
1. Be 25 years old. Both of you.
2. Have known each other for at least ONE FULL YEAR.
3. Have met each other's parents at least twice.
4. Have fully disclosed all finances and financial beliefs about credit, spending, and savings.
5. Have thoroughly disclosed and discussed religious and political beliefs.
6. Have fully discussed and agreed to plans for children. Specifically, how many, when and how to raise them. Also, have had a frank discussion about the fact that you understand that either of you might change your mind later on this.
7. Attended pre-marriage counselling or training of some sort.

If you love each other and are made for each other, you'll still be together when you meet these time frames. You are not fully "you" until you turn 25. You change a lot between 18 and 25. There is a good chance the person you marry at 18 won't be even close to the person you are married to at 25. After 25 the change doesn't stop, but the pace slows, allowing you to grow different together.

Following this advice does not guarantee a great marriage, but it dramatically improves the chances.

On Having Children...

More nagging from my Master Chief's days.

Children are a big deal, and a big responsibility. You OWE it to them to do it right. You CANNOT mess this up!

First of all. You don't have to have children.
Really.
It's not required.

I didn't have children and have never regretted it. Maybe when I'm 80 years old, lonely and in a nursing home I might wish I had them, but I'll have the money I didn't spend on the kid's college to spend on cute nurses (just kidding – but I will be able to afford quality care).

My rules for having children (these assume you are a couple having kids – I don't mean this to be judgmental on single parents).

Before you have children:
1. Be at least 26 years old.
2. Be happily married at least ONE FULL YEAR (if you don't plan on marrying each other for whatever reason be together as you will be as parents for this amount of time).
3. If the marriage is rocky, DON'T HAVE KIDS until you have fixed your marriage.
4. Attend parenting classes.
5. Spend time around kids.
6. Discuss child-rearing philosophy, discipline philosophy, school and college plans, etc.
7. Be financially ready for kids. This means run a real projected budget based on current expenses PLUS kid expenses. Obviously, you can eliminate current expenses like eating out, having fun, seeing movies, or anything else you enjoyed before having kids – because you can kiss all that goodbye! I'm mostly joking, but not really.

Ask for Help if you Need It

Time to get serious…

While the obvious situation would be for academics, that's not what I'm talking about.

I'm talking about when you feel overwhelmed.
I'm talking about when you feel too anxious to leave the house.
I'm talking about when you are depressed, or stressed, or lonely.

All of these feelings are natural, and everyone feels them once and a while, but if you start feeling them all the time, or they start to take over your life, it's time to ask for help.

I'm not an expert on any of this, but I know that these things shouldn't be handled by yourself.

Ask a friend for help.
Ask a family member for help.
Ask an advisor, mentor or supervisor for help.
Get professional help.

If you feel like hurting yourself, don't. Ask for help.
Call 1-800-273-8255 if you can't think of anyone else to talk to.

The one thing not to do is nothing.

Don't Worry About What Other People Think

Wear what you want. Listen to what you want (even country – ew). Be who you want.

Just be nice, and if other people aren't…screw 'em!

You need to make your boss happy. You need to make your parents happy (mostly). You should try to make your significant other and your friends happy, but not at the expense of who you are.

Learning what to give a crap about and what to ignore is one of the hardest, and one of the most important lessons you can learn in life. Most people's opinions you can blissfully ignore. Your appearance (outside of professional requirements) is nobody's business but your own. Don't sweat it. Your opinions, attitude, voice, car choice, friend choice, are also just your business.

Worry less about what people think of you and worry more about being a good person, working hard, having a good attitude and making the world a better place.

If anyone doesn't like it, they can go…well…you know what they can go do.

The World Isn't Falling Apart…

And it isn't ending either.

There's not a lot of money to be made telling everybody that things are fine. News is all about disasters and tragedies and doomsday scenarios.

I've got news for you…

Today, the world is a very good place to live (especially compared to 10, 20 or 50 years ago). Tomorrow, if trends are any predictor of the future, it is going to be even better.

Is everything perfect? No.
Could it be better? Sure.

But let's not believe the hype that everything is awful. You hold in your hand every day the palpable sign of technology improving the world. Your phone can do more, for less money, than the best computers in the world when I was in high school.

World poverty is at an all-time low, and it is only getting better.

We'll figure out this climate change thing – it's what we do. Then we'll move on to the next problem, and solve that one too.

Life is good.
Enjoy it.

www.ingramcontent.com/pod-product-compliance
Lightning Source LLC
Chambersburg PA
CBHW070130240526
45468CB00002BA/761